Church of the Robin's Ha-Ha!

Church of the Robin's Ha-Ha!

John Burroughs' "Natural Religion" and Other Poems

Anne Richey

Epigraph Books
Rhinebeck, New York

Church of the Robin's Ha-Ha!: John Burroughs' "Natural Religion" and Other Poems © 2017 by Anne Richey

All rights reserved. No part of this book may be used or reproduced in any manner without written permission from the author except in reviews and critical articles. Contact the publisher for information.

ISBN: 978-1-944037-78-9
Library of Congress Control Number: 2017951092

Book & cover design by Colin Rolfe
Author photo by Nan Bauer-Maglin

Epigraph Books
22 East Market St., Suite 304
Rhinebeck, NY 12572
(845) 876-4861
www.epigraphps.com

Twill

> *For Nancy Githens Washburn (1944-2002)*
> *— Weaver & friend*

Cat track, snail trail –
we too ply the wild rose path
to the pine tree
and back, intending

this hour for indigo,
the warp in our thoughts leveled,
conceits shed, and sticky egos
dissolved. Walk

at this curiously fallow
time of day, past
querulous cows, and dogs
straining at our scent –

poised and empty,
smiling

at even the unexpected S untwisting
just ahead. There is no web
that can trap us, nor hook
that can hold us apart:

we are nubs
in the emerald algae's
loose weave on the pond,

as much
our neighbor's tabby prowling
the brake as cricket
shuttling through the weedy selvage
of the path.

Our only harness is the breeze.

Contents

I. Church of the Robin's Ha-Ha!

- 3 • Wake-Robin
- 4 • At the Old School Baptist Church, Roxbury NY: Annual Service
- 5 • God?
- 6 • Bait
- 7 • Eggs
- 8 • Hardshell
- 9 • Whittle Stick
- 11 • Rock
- 13 • Sap Bucket
- 14 • Rooster
- 16 • Chill
- 17 • Chunk Stove
- 18 • Nestlings
- 19 • Snake, According to John
- 20 • Hymns
- 22 • Catechism of the Grasses
- 24 • Fledglings
- 25 • Hard Gospels
- 27 • Chance
- 28 • Speckled Trout
- 29 • Snake, According to John
- 30 • John O'Birds
- 31 • Ha! Ha!
- 32 • Green

II. Through a Woman's Eye

- 35 • Three in One
- 37 • Coop
- 39 • Timing

III. Drinking Alone on the Moon

- 45 • Lost Eden
- 47 • Blue-Purple
- 49 • Ashokan Spillway Walk
- 51 • April Smiles
- 52 • Hat-Tipping
- 56 • Drinking Alone on the Moon
- 57 • Tiger Moth
- 59 • On Overlook Mountain with the Rock Reader
- 61 • Walk with Me
- 62 • The Catskills in Winter

IV. Blue Crows

- 65 • The Blasts
- 67 • Infantry
- 68 • Sunset
- 69 • Blue Crows
- 70 • Wild Limb
- 72 • The Falls
- 74 • Whoosh
- 76 • Foolish Child
- 78 • Gossamer

80 • Notes
81 • Acknowledgments
83 • About the Author

I

Church of the Robin's Ha-Ha! John Burroughs' "Natural Religion"

Talk of heaven! ye disgrace earth.
Thoreau

WAKE ROBIN

(Genus Trillium). Blooms in spring. Named for the similarity between its reddish petals and the robin's ruddy breast.

" . . . when I have found the wake-robin in bloom," wrote John, "I know the season is fairly inaugurated."

At the Old School Baptist Church, Roxbury NY: Annual Service

No telling how the deer died – a bear perhaps.
One of ten thousand thousand deaths of its kind.
What little is left lies jumbled in a pile:
brown and white fur in clumps on the grass,
the rib cage stripped clean – surprisingly intact –
and one slender lower leg, still furred
down to its diminutive black hoof.
A young deer like Sabbath-goers generations ago
might have glimpsed through the windows
of this high-storied yellow frame church
nuzzling spring growth among the grave stones
as they sang hymns about the heaven to come.

God?

"I believe God is Nature," John told a friend. "Every day is a Sabbath to me."

Bait

Presumptuous to try to "warp the will of the Lord" –
the Spirit will "nudge" young people to church.
Trust the Spirit, they said.

The Spirit more often nudged John to bathe
in nearby mountain streams, splashing and dunking
in their "dusky, fragrant depths," his boy-heart
storing up hallelujas of delight,

or to fish for trout in a meadow's willow-graced brook
where in shaded pools he found, beneath the trout's
dark top-side camouflage, "glancing iridescent hues,"
more enticing than sermons to "the believing eye":

those sin-obsessed Hardshell sermons, "a curious jumble"
of on-the-spot inspiration – the Elders
"trusting the Lord to put words in their mouths."

Eggs

I was researching the etymology of "wake-robin" in late April, when I looked up from my work table to see a robin land on the deck railing. In her beak a bunch of bleached raffia-like grasses. She'd chosen the flat top of a deck speaker under the roof overhang as the foundation for her nest. Over the next few days, a shallow, loosely-woven rather lopsided nest emerged, with long tendrils trailing from three sides (charming to my eye, but ratifying John's observation that robins aren't always first-rate builders). Construction complete, she laid three blue eggs and sat serene but watchful, day after day, while beneath her soft warm breast unfolded the *mystērium tremendum*.

Hardshell

In the tall air of the yellow church, the visiting Elder noted the tradition of trusting to the Lord for inspiration, and then began to speak. He proclaimed two basic beliefs of the Old School Baptists:

> First, we believe the Lord is our absolute sovereign. Second, we believe in the total depravity of man.

Clearly, the Lord was coherent today.

Whittle Stick

John's father Chauncey –
a square-dealing dairy farmer,
a good man, a righteous man
who had his faults: harsh voiced and hoggish
(at table, spearing the largest potatoes for himself),
hidebound, rude (he never said "thank you"),
a religious bigot.

But *depraved?*

The notion both exasperated John and elicited his pity.

Try dissuading Chauncey.
The cards and whiskey and "naughty ladies"
of his youth . . . He was a son of Iniquity alright.
But *saved*
– no mere child of chance on Nature's firing line –
safe in the arms of the Lord,

one of those heat-of-the-moment folks
(he once prayed on his knees in the hog pen)
believing themselves transformed by Grace,
when "all along," said John, "they had been sound at heart."

"Oh, those poor old souls! But, whatever the significance
of their feeling, it was genuine."

Leave Chauncey and his heretic Methodist neighbor
to their whittle sticks,
let them argue sin and salvation
till the cows come home.

Rock

There's a large rock overlooking a pasture on the Burroughs homestead. On this rock, young John often sat gazing at the low-lying mountains opposite, and daydreaming. Here, perhaps, he intuited the beginnings of his faith – "faith," he said, "founded upon a rock, faith founded in the constitution of things."

Church of blind energy.

Church of the running brooks.

Church of boiling sap.

Church of the robin's Ha-Ha.

Church of 'red in tooth and claw.'

Church of enjoyment.

Church of boyhood.

Church of seed in the wind.

Church of no design.

Church of open-air perfumes.

Church of natural law and order.

Church of mere specks.

Church of the inscrutable universe.

Church of curiosity.

Church of broad daylight.

Church of 'primal sanities.'

Church of the second, third and fourth coming.

Church of the great ice flood.

Church of rocks ground down.

Church of all the time in the world.

Sap Bucket

"The other day in my walk," John told a friend, "I came upon a sap bucket that had been left by the maple tree all the spring and summer. What a bucketful of corruption was that . . . I emptied it upon the ground while I held my nose . . . where I knew every particle of the reeking, fetid fluid would soon be made sweet."

Rooster

In the cemetery next to the yellow church, the deaths of five children from one family are recorded on a single stone.

> ENOS SQUIRE 1
> died Nov. 25 1820 aged
> 1 year 8 mos. 17 days
>
> ENOS SQUIRE 2
> died Feb.23. 1821
> 4 weeks & 5 days
>
> EIDELI 1
> An infant died Dec. 1. 1821
>
> DAVID
> died June 6. 1829 His death
> was produced by being spured
> in the head by a Rooster. aged
> 1 year. 9 mos. & 21 days
>
> ELEANOR
> died April 16. 18 [illegible]
> 11 months & 22 days

Thy will be done?
The Lord is our Absolute Sovereign.

The Nature God, said John, wills nothing.
She is blind, pitiless, her method is hit or miss.
She "hits her mark . . . because she shoots in all directions."

Chill

"I often look back and envy my father the satisfaction he got in his church . . . he didn't feel the great cosmic chill as I feel it. I mean the feeling that comes to one when he sees the tremendous processes of nature go on entirely independent of him, and knows he is not shut in by any protecting walls, that he has . . . to warm himself as best he can."

Chunk Stove

Two of them, actually, midway up the aisles
of the Yellow Church, one on the left, one on the right.

Trim-looking structures, each with a long black spider-
leg duct meeting at the flue behind the pulpit to carry
the smoke away.

(And smoke of another sort some might have joked
after a spirited hell-fire sermon.)

Why "chunk"?
Chunk some more wood for the stove.
Throw another chunk in the stove.

Wood burning for heat, hearts burning for salvation –
just the enveloping warmth folk needed
when sheltered inside from "the cold, drenching
odorless rain of late winter or of March."

Nestlings

Once the baby robins had hatched, the mother continued to warm them, for early May was cool, and they were a vulnerable tangle of sparsely tufted pink-purple nakedness with bulbous lidded eyes. By the third day, there were three fuzzy identifiable nestlings whose tiny heads were mostly beak – usually agape – poking up above the nest's rim eager for a delivery of grub. The interior of their beaks was the beautiful orange-red of the mature robin's breast, but brighter.

Snake, According to John

". . . while strolling through the woods, my attention was attracted to a small densely grown swamp . . . from which proceeded cries of distress and alarm . . . three or four yards from me was the nest, beneath which in long festoons, rested a huge black snake; a bird two-thirds grown was slowly disappearing between his expanded jaws. By slow degrees he compassed the bird in his elastic mouth; his head flattened, his neck writhed and swelled, and two or three undulatory movements of his glistening body finished the work . . .

The parent birds in the meantime kept up the most agonizing cry . . ."

Hymns

After the sermon, the visiting Elder led us in singing "My
 spirit looks to God alone . . ."
My thoughts wandered to young John, fishing on the Sabbath
or tramping over Old Clump,

to his intoxicating revelation that day out rambling
when the "flickering leaves parted"
                              to disclose
the tiny black-throated blue warbler:
". . . the woods we knew so well
held birds, that we knew not at all";

to birds lining out their songs, and his quick notations –
the robin's "Ha-ha! Ha-ha!,"
to John's ears, "the happiest sound
of the whole year";

to his hymns to the "'good in everything' –
in all natural processes and products"

including death,
which he matter of factly observed
was the chemical reduction of the body
to its original elements
by the action of micro-organisms
returning it to earth –

"It is all right," said John's revered friend
and mentor Walt Whitman
as he lay dying:

                "I bequeath myself
to the dirt to grow from the grass I love . . ."

Catechism of the Grasses

What brings a hush to the fields in summer?

. . . the grass, so common, so abundant, so various, a green summer snow that softens the landscape . . .

Why is the cow our "rural divinity"?

She is the true grazing animal. That broad, smooth, always dewy nose of hers is just the suggestion of greensward. She always caresses the grass; she sweeps off the ends of the leaves; she reaps it with the soft sickle of her tongue. She crops close, but she does not bruise or devour the turf . . .

What do we know through her?

What comfort there is in the juicy cud of reverie.

What is the "green inundation"?

. . . behold the meadows with their boundary line of stone fences, that are like lakes and reservoirs of timothy and clover. They are full to the brim, they ripple and rock in the breeze, the green inundation seems about to overwhelm its boundaries, all the surface inequalities of the land are wiped out, the small rocks and stones are hidden, the woodchucks make their road through it, immersed like dolphins in the sea.

What is summer's great delight?

You stoop low. You part away the grass and daisies and would lay bare the inmost secrets of the meadow. Everything is yet tender and succulent; the very air is bright and new; the warm breath of the meadow comes up in your face; to your knees, you are in a sea of daisies and clover; from your knees up, you are in a sea of solar light and warmth.

Fledglings

The mother robin rarely flew straight to the nest – she'd first halt on the deck railing and inspect the vicinity for lurking predators. Once, she arrived while I was sneaking a peek from a ladder I'd placed nearby. She gave me holy hell. Somehow, despite her scolding, she managed to keep a grip on the unlucky worm in her beak. Meanwhile, her babies huddled down in the nest, absolutely still.

Within a week and a half, the nestlings had morphed into gray-brown speckle-breasted juveniles standing tall on sturdy twig legs, flexing their wings. One morning at the end of May, as I climbed the ladder, the largest one panicked and in a burst of wing beats flew up and away. By afternoon, all had fledged.

Hard Gospels

God's grace
– reserved for a predestined few –
was an Old-School Baptist's only ticket
to salvation, a doctrine succinctly articulated
by gunslinger Clint Eastwood:

      "Deserving has nothing to do with it."

In Chauncey's day,
preachers on the Calvinist spectrum
tied themselves into logical knots
trying to explain the paradox of a loving God
who played favorites (yet expected
everyone to be prepared), who deluded
His faithful with false certainty
or tortured them with doubt –
How be confident you were among the Elect?

Many a minister felt duty-bound to offer an assessment.

Groused John: ". . . those people
who know all about God," as if "he lived
around the corner, where they
interviewed him daily."

One wonders if John ever entertained
the uncanny similarity between his Nature God
and his father's God: in the words
of Harriet Beecher Stowe, Nature
was no less an "inexorable Calvinist"
than the God around the corner,
capriciously "selecting"
winners and losers, deserving
or not.

But earth's lowliest worm
(I imagine John's saying)
at least has a fighting chance:
"nature does not take sides."

Chance

"Experimenting and experimenting endlessly, taking a forward step only when compelled by necessity, – this is the way of Nature – experimenting with eyes, with teeth, with limbs, with feet, with toes, with wings, with bladders and lungs, with scales and armors, hitting upon the backbone only after long trials with other forms, hitting upon the movable eye only after long ages of other eyes, hitting on the mammal only after long ages of egg-laying vertebrates, hitting on the placenta only recently, – experimenting all around the circle, discarding and inventing, taking ages to perfect . . ."

Speckled Trout

Be ye a seeker of trout, dark and obscure
but with wondrous tints. Thread your native streams
through the fat and marrowy places of field
and wood. Time yourself to their meandering –
stopping to gaze upon the spotted lily.
Blend with the trees and the shadows.
Mark the meadow brooks' every glance
and dimple, how they burrow under the roots
of great willows, pause and pool at the foot
of moss-covered rocks – how the trout tarry
under high cool banks, half hiding to lurk
and spring for prey. Press on through brush
and briars, past the whistling wings
of the 'dropping snip' into the deep woods –
where the trout are black, and blacker still
the shadows under the hemlocks, all gloom
and silence. Savage, uncompromising.
Yield ye to the fascination, penetrate farther
towards the center of the mystery. Sit ye hidden.
Hunger whetted, bait your hook with the quick
and the fresh. Bait it with your heart.

Snake, According to John

"Whether we call it snake or devil matters little. I could but admire his terrible beauty . . . his black shining folds, his easy gliding movement, head erect, eyes glistening, tongue playing like a subtle flame, and the invisible means of his almost winged locomotion."

"The devil . . . is part of the Eternal Good. I want no emasculated universe. I want the fiber and virility and pungency and power and heat and drive which all that we call bad gives it."

John O' Birds

"Accident and destruction and death are nothing to Nature," John reminded us. Indeed, most baby robins don't survive the first year. Yet, I rarely look out my windows without seeing an adult robin or two or three or four skittering over the yard or taking a dip in the birdbath. Perhaps the two dousing themselves yesterday were my youngsters – enthusiastic self-baptizers, taking turns, smacking the water with their wings.

Ha-Ha!

After the service, I shook hands with the Elder, then wandered over to the cemetery where several robins flitted among the graves. A female touched down on a head stone. I hoped she'd indulge me with "Ha-ha! Ha-ha!" – but she had her own agenda and quickly flew away. After all, Nature did not make the robin to sing for us. But she did make us (careful with that word "make") to sing its praises, and to ponder the wherefore of our delight.

Green

Up the road from the Burroughs homestead,
in a weedy nook by a bend, lies an old burying ground,
a jumble now of weathered stones. Among the few
legible names is *Rebecca*, who "departed this life"
at nineteen. Silvery lichens edge her stone like lace
scallops on a dress she might have dreamed of,
breaking from her chores to rest against a tree –
as her stone rests now against this tree. How she died
is lost to time, but that she died so young –
in those days, no surprise. *Gone to a better place.*
Better than here, where high above her grave
her hair is turning green?

II

Through a Woman's Eye

Three in One

– A Lena Underwood Photograph

Had the house gone suddenly quiet – her sons
still inside? Did she grab her camera (they were favorite subjects),
and tiptoe room to room
until – *ah, perfect!*

They're boy-worlds away on the parlor sofa,
reading a magazine with apparently magnetic properties.

The older boy, in sturdy lace-up shoes, braces his feet
at sofa's edge, propping it on his knees; the younger,
legs crossed grown-up style, lends a finger-tip
assist (the cover is floppy) as if shy
to assert the necessity.

Their naturalness attests to Lena's finesse,
and a telling deference,
for their faces, half-concealed behind the magazine,
suggest murmurous deep discussion.

On the wall, right above them, hang two framed photos:
one of a cherry tree, its blossoms, says the text,
hand-tinted by Lena (pink's my guess, but in this black & white,
they're whitish);

the other, a print of the boys just past cherub stage
with a scrubbed-up-for-the-sitting-look,
posed as if conjoined at the shoulders, heads tipped,
touching, tiny handkerchiefs poking
from the pockets of identical suits, like petals.

Did Lena tint this one? Say she did, say she pinked their cheeks,
say she was thinking how fugitive those blossoms.

(for Luke and Jeb)

Coop

– An Anna Carroll Photograph

"Don't move," Anna Carroll must have said to the two
young sisters in this circa 1900's black & white –
who, unlike David, the Roxbury tot killed by a rooster
in 1829, look to be on amicable terms with their fowl
(no dust up in the littered yard of the coop),

                         the solemn older girl standing

school-marmish in her stiff A-line skirt and high-
collared blouse, left arm clutching a hen to her chest.
Its witchy claws dangle below her belt – or above,
if, head under a black cloth, you are striving to focus
an image that's upside down. But there's a blur
where the hen

(or is it a rooster?) pecks at feed in the girl's right hand,
though the wing-like bow in the girl's up-swept hair
is notably crisp (like the stop-motion of a bird about
to lift off) and her expression is sharp. Yes, it says,
I'll pose with the chickens, but I'd like
to get to town,

                   or some such sufferance, perhaps

a concession to her younger sister whose eyes
have a hint of triumph as she extends her cupped palm
to the camera, displaying a bitty nestled there.
She's pushed her sleeves to the elbow, but seems
untroubled by the dirt she's kneeling in – her dress,
a loose-fitting print,

must be filthy at the hem. No surprise her own bird-wing
bow's a little ragged. It's endearing how, in a speckled
hen way, the print of the dress links her to the big-
bosomed birds around her, as if she's the sister with
the brooding instinct – an early bloom of maternal
delight in her face,

                        a love for small fated things.

Timing

– Two Edna Benedict Photographs

1.

Try to see Edna Benedict, née Georgia,
lugging her tripod to this sweat-of-the brow-place,
this field scythed to a rough-cut clearing

where her father Andrew and brother Wendell
have forked a load of hay onto their mule-drawn wagon;

to see her leveling the tripod's long legs
on the stubby ground, topped (if it didn't topple)
with the glass plate camera;

now, father, reins in hand, standing center load
in the posture of a charioteer, the hay
spilling over the wagon's side like a great
unkempt mustache; his face, straw-hat-shaded,
a smudge compared to brother's,

which is lit by the sun. Perched on the wagon's
far side, Wendell faces Edna. Still, his boyish features
are hard to read. The family prankster (we're told).
Is he grinning? One wants a magnifying lens to see.

Think of it: that era gone like mist, yet we have
the benefit of Edna's eyes, though not
her pleasant dim awareness of the hay-scented air,
the stubble resisting the soles of her shoes –

focus and exposure uppermost in her mind,
her glass plate sessions recalled as "solemn times"
by those she admonished not to smile.

2.

Don't smile! – probably a challenge for Wendell.
By the time of this later portrait – he sits in a chair
in a flower-strewn meadow – Edna may have adopted
the Kodak Brownie, for he does smile ("you press
the button, we do the rest") free to look
more like himself.

You could say it's one of those Kodak-touted "moments" –
or, as Joseph Lux argued back then in the "Is-this-art?" debate:
"snapshots" give us "pictures of the soul."

Only shaggy Prince, his dog, looks somber.

It's 1915, Wendell's about twenty
in shirt and tie, striped wool suit; clean-shaven,
square chinned, hair fashionably parted a tad off center –
likely just back from the Methodist church,
soon joking at the Sunday table. With his legs
casually crossed and his dog by his side, you'd think him
to the manor born. Here in this remote bucolic setting

(where exactly is West Meredith?), he rivals
the era's young lords of the Hudson in confident ease,
and in some bright intangible – is it optimism?

Ah, Wendell Georgia, apple of the camera's eye –
Edna has preserved your perfection
in a country on the brink: "the war to end all wars."

Yet look at you: you smile and smile
as if news of the fallen world had never reached you.

III

Drinking Alone on the Moon

Lost Eden

> *– 11 hamlets erased by the construction*
> *of the Ashokan Reservoir, 1907 - 1915.*

Locomotives, steam shovels,
stone crushers, dump wagons,
boilers, traction engines, drills,
pumps. 200 mules, their skilled
Black handlers. Picks, axes,
chisels, saws. Hand-savvy
Swedes, Poles, Russians, Danes,
Germans, Irish, Canadians,
Englishmen, Austrians, Italians –
oh, a veritable Little Italy:
gelato, mandolins, bocci balls,
cockfights, the wet-flour scent
of pasta drying on fences.
Locals, too: one, Elwyn Davis,
keen diarist & weather recorder:
Nasty squally raw.
Fired traction engine 10 hours.
. . . fever, feel tough all over.
Great change on Sand Hill
from cemetery to RR bed.
2700 exhumed, re-located.
Frazzled diggers snoozing

in coffins – and did you hear:
one digger, irked by his wife's
yak-yak, re-interred her late
husband (Mr. Perfect, apparently)
standing on his head!
Brush, trees, stumps, homes,
schools, shops, farms, barns,
mills, creameries, maple-
shaded streets, boarding houses,
porch swings, flagstone walks,
someone's prize rose bushes
(not even a how-do-you-do!)
razed, grubbed, dumped,
burned, blasted. The dam:
earth, stone & cement.
Venerable paths, trout-quick
streams – where now?
Twist of a valve, city hurrahs.
Upstate, stunned & stricken souls,
a woman mourning her roses.

Blue-Purple

In September,
> for five to six weeks at most,

a bounty in Adams' market bins

> of small blue-purple, egg-shaped plums
with delicate cloud-veils

rubbing won't clear,
nor washing.

Not that one wants such loveliness
> to disappear – it's just

when the eye wonders about surface
or depth,

> there's a compulsion to test.

The slow cook-
> down of plums to jam (the unpeeled

> > plums halved and pitted,

dumped in a pot
with water to cover, lemon, cinnamon and sugar)

leaves no trace of blue or purple,
                                  much less

            cloud unless
you count escaping steam.

                  But ladling the thick brown jam
                  from the pot, it came to me

(I actually said "oh")

                      that memory is a kind of thrift:
the blue-purple I couldn't put up in jars.

Ashokan Spillway Walk with Alice G.

1. By the reservoir we stop for the view.
   Blue mountains rim the horizon.
   Their overlapping slopes are soft,
   inviting as women. "Voluptuous," you say.
   "Bella," I say, and see an Italian
   stop his pickax midair.

2. A lone rowboat floats on their placid reflection.
   It's no bigger than an eyelash from here.
   In the stillness, our breathing slows.
   A thousand eras lost to wind, and still
   the great sages all share this moment.
   Li Po, is that you beside us?

3. Walking on, our talk turns to male-female.
   You say: Language makes them opposites.
   "Yes," I say, "but our hearts give the lie to duality."
   I was thinking of Li Po, away from home
   longing for his kids: *Who comforts them*
   with loving hugs now?

4. A diving bird distracts us.
    We watch the water ripple then resolve
    into smoothness under the sinking sun.
    Will it re-surface? In the half-dark,
    the water seems all possibility.
    So it is with the ten thousand things.

April Smiles

A frog sings for love down by the pond,
twanging like a taut rubber band.
A yard man whistles as a girl walks by.
Pastel eggs adorn a budding bush.
Even I have dyed my hair.

Hat-Tipping

> – *from the diary of Katherine Scudder, Roxbury NY*
> *(May-June, 1899)*

Made a cream cake (scorched it). I bought a pair of shoes for $1.40, and had to exchange them for Abe had given me one 5 and one 6. I got only two tips today . . .

Heard Mr. Mattice preach twice – morning subject "For what is your life" – evening "2 heavens" . . . I shook hands with him for the first time after cutting nails 7 Sundays . . .

Swept schoolhouse, was quite cranky all day, nothing of importance happened, fooled with the children instead of studying . . . Bought a quart of onions for 10 cents. John Morse walked from Hubbells store down with Ola. Emma and I had fun with them. We attended the meeting, the boys walked up the hill together and so did the girls, and when they stopped to say goodnight, we stopped too – just for fun I guess.

I had quite an accident while dressing this morning, raised my arm to pin my collar and my sleeve ripped halfway out. Just as I was going to empty the water with the pail in my hand Levi and the two Vega boys came past, I did not dare look up for some time, and when I did, Sollie was still looking and gave me a tip. I went to the Baptist church, and Eva and I quarreled over Fred . . . Met Riley; he asked me why I never came over (he did not tip), and next I met a teacher, he did tip, always does . . .

Taught school as usual. After school I walked to H'ville to get the examinations which had not been sent to me. Mary and Rose had been "wheeling." At P.O. got my 25th tip. Spent the evening in reading, music and visiting. Wanted to finish a chapter in my room but got scared over the lamp and extinguished it just on the point of exploding and had quite a time going to bed in the dark . . .

Went to the village with Rose, and she went with me to the Library. I exchanged "Last of the Mohicans" for Franklins Autobiography. Got 7 tips . . .

I taught school, swept the floor and blistered my hands. Had the sick headache when I reached home . . . I worried over my [examination] essay, and in the afternoon, I went down to take English history, when the fire bell rang you should have seen us jump from our seats to the aisle and the window. I went home for supper after which I went to prayer meeting. When we reached Roxbury, a hail and thunderstorm had reached there too, some hailstones reached three inches in circumference. Got 9 tips – 41 in all . . . I did miserable work reading my essay, but got my diploma just the same, it was an eventful day, but it is over now and I am glad . . .

Went home with May Hull. She and I went to take a walk and we saw Philo with a red hat on. We did not speak to him . . . There was no school today, for it was the day Mabel was buried, she was laid out in a white dress, white stockings and white slippers, she had a beautiful white casket, and John Hubbell preached a sermon which seemed to me cold and heartless . . .

Taught school again today I felt like crying every time I looked at Mabel's seat . . .

Nothing of importance to write about today except getting vaccinated by Dr. Cartwright. John and I started after black raspberries but finding them scarce, we filled our pails from the billberry tree . . . I churned this morning, the first time in over a year. 1 tip (46). Mary Powell said she would never have her picture taken in groups with Myron. I would not go quite so far as that.

Drinking Alone on the Moon

Every step rebuffed.
Dust, craters, rocks as far as eye can see.
Earth's breezes waft across memory
like the musk of a departed lover.
I tilt the bottle again.
I look my fill beneath her blue-white gauzes,
lay my head on her greening slopes.
It is spring in the Catskills, season of sighs.
I raise my cup to burgeoning buds.
and say, Li Po, a little more wine
and the Star River will take you home
where pond frogs call to one another,
and the moon silvering night
keeps its distance.

According to legend, Li Po drowned when he fell from a boat, drunkenly trying to embrace the moon. I decided to give him his moon.

Tiger Moth

> *– Hence, I say the way of knowledge of Nature*
> *is the way of love . . .*
>
> John Burroughs

Wooly bears are crossing the road
– it's tempting to say with a will –
the road that runs by the old Burroughs
farm, woodland on either side.

On cool autumn days, John would've
seen these bristly bands
– black, orange-brown, black –
inching from coming cold toward clefts

in rocks, bark-encrusted crevices
in logs. Why cross at all? You'd
have to be at ground level to know.
John hit the same road at 17,

to the consternation of his father
who couldn't fathom an oilskin satchel
packed for a life of learning
(John's instincts the soulful sort).

In this slant October sun,
the wooly bears' gait makes fluttering
wing-shadows of their bodies,
like templates for spring's unfurling

when, tiger moths at last, winged
& yellowish & horny, they'll have
a few days to mate before they die.
John wasted no time himself

on that score, but widening his embrace,
he took to the woods where
intimacy, he said, grew with the seasons.
You can still hear his amorous roar.

On Overlook Mountain with the Rock Reader

1.

On the summit, our fingers trace
faint lines in ice-age stone. The rock reader
drops to his knees and flattens his palms –
inches forward, releases, inches forward:
how a massive glacier wrote those lines
groaning, creaking as it advanced.

2.

You'd paint us small on this out-cropping:
one step more, we'd drop sky-deep
to the valley below. Where an ice-sheet once
ground south, the breath of summer rises
now, and the Hudson basks like a snake
in the sun.

3.

Our feet scuff names and dates on rock
incised by hikers a century ago.
Immortality on Overlook! someone says.
The rock reader laughs, points north
where clouds skim hills once high
as the Himalayas.

Walk with Me

Mountain whimsy:
a faded dinghy
moored in a sea of billowing grasses.

*

My neighbor's swayback mare
– a rescue –
flat on her side in the snow,
sunbathing.

*

Corn field slashed to stubble.
Crow-gleaners,
placid as grazing cows.

The Catskills in Winter

Exit Lowe's, and there they are, bluntly
notching the horizon, thickset and muscular –
a squat solidity that tugs at my eyes and
brings me to a standstill. It makes me want

to be Cezanne off in a corner of the parking lot
studying the hunched contours the cold's exposed,
daubing pigments wintry as smoky quartz
on canvas. Winter works a forever-kind-of-look

on these mountains which hides their transience.
This lot even, once the site of an ancient inland sea
with tree-high ferns along the shore, is now a frozen
lake of asphalt filled with cars. Cezanne,

perched across from Mont Sainte-Victoire
knew the latest theories of earth's great shifts,
but his mind's eye, fastened on the underlying
forms in nature, told him *something* lasts.

I could stand here all day trying to see it.

IV

Blue Crows

The Blasts –

gas canisters blowing at random in a field of corn
to frighten crows – were trifling compared to those
in places where people are lucky not to die. Still,
unsettling. I was into my blessings count –
these days practically a reflex –

when a bulky shadow up ahead cut me short: a dog,
a big black dog, sprawled on the shoulder of the road,
neck hyper-extended, head flattened between
his paws, & a rigidity suggesting "petrified"
in both its senses.

You'd think a Doberman would at least bark.
I stroked his head, but his eyes stayed locked
on something only he could see. At a loss
(car a mile away, no phone, & rows of corn
like prison bars), I knelt,

began to massage him neck to rump, long deliberate
strokes at first, then languid as the sun rose hotter.
Somewhere I'd seen a soldier's "selfie" – just a kid
really, grinning beside a pile of rubble. "Luck's
holding," he'd texted.

Given the daily carnage, what mother would
dare to tell him (much less herself) Luck
has no memory? The "ceasefire" in the corn field,
when it came, was a slow revelation of country
silence, broken at length

by an approaching car. A stranger I'd have to trust.
He knew the dog's owner. With a quiet "Okay, fella,"
he lifted him into the car. *You?* Thanks, no, I said,
patting the Doberman goodbye. I needed to walk,
make what peace I could.

Infantry

Rows of corn –
not "flaggy" now,
but brown and stiff.
From their stalks
leaves dangle
like rusty swords.
Of the crowds
of blooms
that cheered
on the roadside
all summer, only
blighted goldenrod
waves now.
Red oaks bleed
at the field's edge.
Havoc that will soon
lie under snow,
stubs of stalks
poking through.
Winter's end,
they'll be plowed under.
Hard on their heels
green thousands . . .
the same marching orders.

Sunset

On the far side of the pasture my neighbor's horse
stands so still, I think: this is not repose—
her muscles are too tensed, her gaze too fixed—this
is attention: she's watching the sun's soundless slide
to the horizon. I've brought an apple, but reluctant
to intrude, toss it hand to hand. What I see is a huge
blood-orange thing burning in the sky. It looms like
an eye that sees but does not see, like Death before
a harvest. If her world is kinder than ours, if she
does not shiver at this sight--and her stillness says not—
then what is this sunset to her? All I know is what I
selfishly wish: radiance with no name, simple silence.

Blue Crows

The field is rough and choppy from the plow.
The way the morning sun silvers it,
the man and his dog appear to walk on water.
I slow down, enjoying their saunter
as wavelets lap their feet. When the driver
behind me honks his impatience,
I wave him around. You can't hurry glory.
Later I tell my son, who says once
he saw crows made blue by the light.

Wild Limb

> – *There is another world, and it is in this one.*
> *Paul Eluard*

When he stepped to the deck,
they scattered –
              but not far.

I don't bite, he whispered,
and, propping his elbows on the railing,
lost himself in their quiet drift.

A crash in the woods, a trio of strained
unlovely wheezes: vowelly long deep-throated
rasps, one after the other, then
more or less in unison.

As if to drive their message home,
the big one stamped the ground, its right foreleg
hinging/un-hinging
like a dancer's mime of a wind-up toy.
When the others followed suit,
why, he can't say, but he did too –

left leg in the air
with a mind of its own.

Then some tacit *all clear*, the deer began
to melt away.

Did his feet even touch the ground?

The Falls

> *A Georgia man hiking in dress shoes . . . died*
> *Saturday after falling about 60 feet onto rocks*
> *below.*
> The Daily Freeman

> *. . . there are danger signs everywhere.*
> Online comment

The man who wore dress shoes to his death
hadn't planned it that way,
but with the roar of the falls in his ears,
shoes may have seemed
a minor consideration, if one at all.

Awful, we say – meaning it, of course –
and would move on to other news
but for the shoes:
black we presume, smooth soled, buffed earlier
to a shine. So right for some formal occasion.

Still, he'd made it to the top – a wing-tipped
"in spite of" (though we assume he took the safer trail).
It's the "because of" coming down which
gives us pause: the shoes, for sure,
                                         but also

the choice to descend
by that off-trail path signs warned against,
suggesting a more perilous terrain inside his head,
the slipperiest, perhaps, of all.

Whoosh

With a feet forward *whoosh*, wings
power-braking in a downward flare,
the hawk landed spot-on

at the base of a mulched maple,
not six feet from where we'd frozen
on the road, and, righting himself

on staunch legs, loomed
over that small realm, tracking the stir
beneath: some dim, anonymous

thumb-sized thing – a mouse? a vole? –
had run for cover, and now shifting
rumples were all the hawk

could see, his head at a quizzical tilt
as he picked at the undulant grasses.
He never looked our way.

Such pure rapacity . . .
That part of me drilled in distance
allowed the hawk was

simply hungry; a step farther
back, it recognized a little life
deluded by mere straw.

Foolish Child

My hosta, a forest now
of naked stalks. Worse, the lilies
bordering the road: Magritte-weird,
like a row of neatly beheaded
parade goers. I'd been suckered:
all those weekend bike trips up here
before I fled the city, when deer
in the fields batted their big eyes
my way to watch me watch them,
eyes that seemed to question everything
and nothing, bodies statue-still
as long as I matched their stillness.
Who knew their ears were so elegant
with velvet-trim, their tails so pert?
On bummed-out city days, it had
amused me to conjure five or six
drifting across 5th Avenue, east-side
chic, as if taxis and trucks were
flocks of starlings. Well, I'm over that.
Earlier today, a trio of them dis-
patching the lilies around my new
mailbox. A hail of stones scattered
them with a scramble of legs and snap
of twigs I relished. What to do?
Some nasty smelly stuff—bobcat urine

(*bobcat urine?*), garlic oil – or,
somewhere I'd read, human hair?
Dammit, maybe a fence. Just how
high was what I was pondering
when I saw the doe, hugely pregnant,
reclining on the ridge – god knows
how long she'd been there – gazing at me
with a patient-mother-look of such
bottomless knowing it almost
caved my knees.

Gossamer

> *– To be is to be perceived.*
> Bishop Berkeley

A windless day when I saw it: a web
like a flag at the top of a metal post, unfurled and taut.

From where I stood, the daylight moon – it hung
above the cornfield across the road – seemed
snagged in the web. Such an anemic splotchy thing,
it appeared the spider had sucked it dry.

I was looking for the rigging – what held the web
aloft – when the sun revealed a filament
like a length of wire pulled tight,
angling towards the ground, down, down,
until midway, in the shade of a bordering thicket,
it became invisible.

The slant of the silk suggested anchorage
in a tangle of ferns, but for the *nothing* I could see,
it ended mid-air: a hostage to shade,
and, with a nod to the bishop, my eyes,

The moon by now had been scavenged
by the sky. I never saw the spider.
But the web, I can vouch –

the web held fast, somehow.

Notes

Roxbury, NY's Old School Baptist Church, also known as the Yellow Church, is on the National Register of Historic Places. Regular services are not held anymore, but once a year a visiting Elder presides over a service that is open to the public.

"Speckled Trout" is a "found poem" derived from the first pages of John Burroughs' essay of the same name.

The four poems in Section II, *Through a Woman's Eye*, are based on photographs in *Through a Woman's Eye: Pioneering Photographers in Rural Upstate* by Diane Galusha with Karen Marshall.

"Lost Eden" draws on three sources: *The Last of the Handmade Dams: The Story of the Ashokan Reservoir* by Bob Steuding; *West Shokan: The Eden of the Catskills* by Elwyn Davis; and the journals of Davis, a resident of West Shokan at the time of the Ashokan Reservoir construction.

"Hat-Tipping" is a "found poem." Katherine Scudder's diary is available in the Roxbury Library's history archives.

Chinese poet Li Po (701-762 C.E.) wrote during the Tang Dynasty.

Acknowledgments

Appalachian Heritage: "Twill"
Chronogram: "Ashokan Spillway Walk with Alice G.," "The Catskills in Winter," "The Falls"
Roanoke Review: "Sunset"
Snowy Egret: "Blue Crows"
WaterWrites: A Hudson River Anthology: "On Overlook Mountain with the Rock Reader"
Universe at Your Door: The Slabsides Poets: "Drinking Alone on the Moon"

Some of those poems have been modified since their original publication.
Most of the poems in this book were in process over the past year and a half and appear here for the first time.

Poet Terese Svoboda's critical eye improved these poems over many bouts of give and take. Bless Terese for her phenomenal patience. Alice Greenwood and Naomi Rothberg gave several of these poems close readings and offered valuable insights. Bill Birns and Diane Galusha, activists and educators in the cause of John Burroughs, kindly read and commented on Parts I and II, respectively. Family members

– Russ, Jon and Nikii – attended to various aspects of this book and contributed their respectable two cents.

Essays by Professor Daniel G. Payne (SUNY-Oneonta) on Burroughs' "natural religion" both inspired and informed me. The Roxbury Library and the Olive Free Library alerted me to Burroughs resources at their sites and online; and the Hurley Library issued special book orders. Paul Cohen and Colin Rolfe of Epigraph Publishing Service (with an emphasis on *service*) provided quality advice essential to my first book endeavor. The specifically Burroughs poems in this volume would not have happened without Rich Parisio, who organized the Slabsides Poets' meet-ups at the John Burroughs Nature Sanctuary.

I am deeply grateful to them all.

Finally, I am the beneficiary of many glorious porch-sitting days at Woodchuck Lodge where Burroughs often sat and wrote. Reveling in the big blue skies and the mountains across the way, listening to the robins, keeping an eye out for porcupines and woodchucks, not to mention the many interested visitors to the Lodge – who could not feel appreciation for the youth who discovered there was "news in every bush" and for the old man whose last words on a train somewhere in Ohio were, "How far are we from home?"

About the Author

Anne Richey lives and teaches in New York's Hudson Valley. She was introduced to John Burroughs through the Slabsides Poets, a writers' group which met periodically at Slabsides, Burroughs' cabin in West Park, NY. She has been reading, studying, and teaching him ever since. Her poems have appeared in numerous journals, among them *Barrow Street*, *Poetry Midwest*, *Primavera*, *Long Island Quarterly*, *The Sow's Ear*, and *JAMA*. They have been anthologized in the collections *Prima Materia*, *Vanguard Voices of the Hudson Valley*, *WaterWrites*, *A Slant of Light: Contemporary Women Writers of the Hudson Valley*, and *Boomer Girls: Poems from the Baby Boom Generation*. She is a docent at Woodchuck Lodge, Burroughs' summer retreat in Roxbury, NY.

www.ingramcontent.com/pod-product-compliance
Lightning Source LLC
Chambersburg PA
CBHW020949090426
42736CB00010B/1332